The Best Version

of You

Robert Moran
Michael Pampena
Andrew Lackey

ISBN 978-1-0827-5575-0 (paperback)
www.SelfRichLife.com

CHAPTER 1

A Fresh Start

Why is this book worth your time? Times are great and you are as financially stable as you have ever imagined. Business is booming and politics is at a healthy state. The entire world lives in peace and life is just as we expected.

For this book to work, let's just pretend that the world is falling apart (literally like the earth is dying). Pretend that we are a country that gets along and is not divided over what politician will make them rich. First, we need you to answer this important question, the question that will decide if this book is truly for you. You must dig deep to answer this question. There is no age requirement or socioeconomic status.

So to start, why is any of this necessary? All we care about is getting you to ask yourself this: have you ever taken a chance on yourself? Have you ever just took complete control of your life and went all in on your dreams?

If not, maybe it is not too late for this to happen. The chances are that you have accepted the conditions of a life that is almost what you wanted, but you fell just short. The fact is, you may be closer than you think. You do not have to start over. You may just need to re-adjust.

Most people only see the world through a very narrow window. What if the struggles that appear everyday can actually result in a better future? It is not impossible, nor crazy. Times have changed but the same problems keep arising. Simply put: are you in control of your freedom, happiness, and money?

If you took every major problem and looked at the very root of what is trying to be accomplished, you will see that it is more money in the pockets of struggling people. In addition, it includes getting a better standard of living for every person.

This begins with a better education. Are we getting the right education? A better job with more money seems to be the solution, but many disagree on how to get there. It has now turned way more personal and political than it needs to be. The idea that is taught to us growing up is to groom another employee.

Unfortunately, this leads to people changing themselves for others' satisfaction. We essentially change who we are because we cannot rely on ourselves for a good life. This leads to a life that has little freedom and happiness, that depreciates every day. Let's first look at the major problem haunting the country today.

While many have short term solutions, we need an investment for a better long term solution. The way this traces back into the business world is that we need less employees and more entrepreneurs. For now, we are going to focus on why this even matters and how we can solve it.

In reality, the majority of the world dreams of self-sufficient individuals. If one were to really think about where this world is headed, self-sufficiency is becoming our only hope.

We are seeing a time when business, and now even government, cannot help us. This has resulted in much of the turmoil we see today, coming from poverty, and resulting into crime. If we are to actually live in this ideal world, we must first address how we have to get there.

This involves admitting to ourselves that we, and only we, have the key to our own life. Initiate this task by taking the root of it. It goes as follows. You must become self-rich mentally before you can become self-rich financially. It truly starts with us. Looking into the mirror and admitting that a change has to happen due to our failed ways is audacious. Breaking from that comfortable life is never easy. As you will see, you start to break away from the norm and what others expect for your own life.

Before you even begin, first understand who we are writing this book for. This is for the poor-minded. Of course, many people are not willing to admit they are poor-minded, we certainly were not. For those who cannot admit that, ask yourself if you are truly happy and free in life. If not, maybe this book is just for you.

For those who doubt self-help, just know this is self-respect, not help. We are not telling you that this is our idea or to try our strategies, but rather that this is what we all have deep down. If you still do not believe us or how we can help, do us one little favor. Read the book. After you have opened your mind to the ideas, it's time to think: were you actually poor minded?

At the rate we are going, we're headed towards another recession, one that might be even worse than the Great Depression. We require less division in our politics, our communities, and our daily lives. It is going to take all that we are and all that we are made of. We need to be rich in two ways, spiritually and financially. Spirituality will make us mentally rich, and it is only when we are mentally rich that we become financially rich. Life can be hard and unfair. Actually, life IS hard and unfair. We can make it better, even if it's not ground-shattering. We must accept change because the change the world needs, lies in us.

The demand right now is not found in our schools or politicians. It lies in the deepest part of who we are. The perspective we view ourselves is going to come out in how we view the world. There is a demand for change in the way we view the world because the way we view ourselves is extremely poor and we express that into the real world. We hide behind our ideas, our theories, and our political affiliations. The truth is out there for us all to know. The solution is out there. We must search for it ourselves and be more independent. The solution lies only in the self, and only when you can become mentally and financially rich, can you survive.

For those that think they are rich, keep one thing in mind. You are only as financially stable as you would be during a recession. In the modern world with modern problems, this recession that we speak of can happen in the near years. If you are not in control of your income or of your life, you will fall victim to the dreaded trap just as easily as everyone else, especially the ones people often look down on.

This is the one thing that unites those that make the minimum-wage and those that work for an employer that pays at a much higher rate. In this day and age with the value of a dollar becoming almost nothing. Of course before we can ever understand that at a later time, we must first know that we have contributed to the problems of today just as much as the ones we blame.

As the government just prints money at the rate that they do, how could money hold any value? Money is nothing anymore, and the rich have discovered this, and it is why they keep getting richer while the ones who fail to see this continue to fall into poverty. Money is only used for building assets, not saving.

We have directed our valuable time and attention to a few areas of topic. We have searched in politics and education reform to decide our fate. It all masks the real problem at hand. The idea of the rich getting richer and the poor getting poorer is not new and just thought of, nor is the demand for better politicians and better education. An inexpensive education will not do as much we would like to believe. For a child coming from an underprivileged family, learning business and money will be stronger for their future than a college education, even a free one for that matter. This is not all about money or being wealthy. While those concepts are a large part of why entrepreneurs take their jump, they are widely misunderstood. The money creates a lifestyle that gives us the greatest life we could ask for. Money is essential in order to be able to give back to those in need and to provide your family a life they ultimately never had. Unfortunately, many corrupt and greedy people in our world make money seem evil and cynical.

The power of observation. We all do it, but in different ways. We have noticed something that many evil and rich people lack. A sense of self-love. The way we view ourselves, and the way we love ourselves is just as important as the money that we have in our pockets.

It is not that cumbersome. We will not go into great detail into money until we go into great detail as to how we need to view ourselves.

Perhaps the reason so many people are unhappy, mentally and financially, is because for too long we have been incorrectly addressing these issues. Of course, this is hardly the majority fault. For years, in one way or another, we have been misguided. Although, sometimes with good intentions. It really leaves us with a simple question, who has been guiding our path?

The only way to view this question is with an outside perspective. While that may sound strange, let's think of the emotional and egotistical way we travel through life. We have been given identities to divert us from the truth, peace, and wealth. How do we release our identities, drop our political views, and just be individuals wanting to succeed in life?

It is not intricate and has been done for years with various individuals in different generations. Those that take the free and independent path typically lead the greater life, mentally and financially.

As a human race, we have reached a point in our society in which politics and identities are taking over. Very few of us are individuals, but rather just a member of another group. This given identity has caused a divide in this country that ultimately makes very little to no sense. There is more than one reason as to why the rich are getting richer and the poor are getting poorer, and it lies within the culprit itself, money.

In order to see this view, in order to comprehend the broad picture, you we must drop any and all political affiliations or identities that the media has created for us. Then, remind yourself that we are individuals with a passion for learning, with our own individual passions and desires. As humans, we enjoy differing ideas and concepts than our peers. Taking your own course in life, facing difficulty or with ease, can lead to a successful life. It is during this time where much depression looms, (both mentally and financially) that these values stand most efficient. Bringing out the best in ourselves requires restructure. We like to believe most of us can agree on this idea.

As to where and what we restructure, is where disagreement may form. With the growing income inequality and elevated student debt, a low number of us see any hope for where their lives are headed. When the government prints more money and uses it for higher education, these institutions will continue to get more expensive. It is only a matter of time before the student debt bubble explodes.

Along with the previously stated idea, globalization and outsourcing of jobs has caused workers to fear for their futures, but more importantly, their source of income. It is not just manufacturing jobs that are departing. Professions such as lawyers and accountants are now losing their positions in a field that was once considered "safe." As more and more jobs are proving that employees are not needed as much as they once were, entrepreneurship seems to be the more promising route.

Now, this is knowledge that is not taught in schools. Think about your classes in high school, middle school, and even elementary school. What were you taught? What types of ideas were the main focus and importance? Schools in the United States do not possess classes that will teach its students money and entrepreneurship because they are not designed to. The phrase "this world is changing" is commonly heard in conversation and in the media. It is a true statement. Entrepreneurship is the new demand.

It is why so many in the new rich category do not even attend school. As schools get more expensive with very little payoff, the new rich are searching for wealth in other places, starting with knowing change will only come from the self. Proven by earlier experiences in history, there are plenty of examples of great leaders and figures in history that succeeded in the worst times this country has ever seen.

You're not reading just another book worshipping money, but we do care about that once we have searched for freedom and happiness without it.

Remember, there is no financial prosperity until there is a mental richness. Therefore, this requires us to take an exceptionally deep look at how we view ourselves. Before you ever lead your dream life with financial stability, we must first accept that we can conquer that life. The great lifestyle you live must first come from a place of deep love for the self.

You must first learn to love yourself. You must first learn to know yourself as well. From our own experiences and scenarios dealt with, we have realized that very few actually put their self first. The simplest understanding of this is happiness. We generally tend to please others at our expense. This leads us down a path where we live lives that please others while we stay put. Our true potential never fully put forth.

There is a demand for change in the way we view the world. We have poor attitudes to ourselves and how we look at ourselves. This leads to explain how we treat others, spreading around toxic air. This toxic air that surrounds us is expressed into the real world.

It is direct and straightforward. We hide behind our ideas, in our theories, and in political affiliations. The truth and the solution lies only in the self. When you can become mentally rich, you will then have the ability to become financially rich.

Those of us that are safe are the ones that have the truth or facts. It also requires the accurate education. We talk a great deal about a better education but we miss the point. Education needs work, but being better sort of misses the point. Education needs a change, it needs a new direction. Times have changed, but education has not. It has gotten so poor that we are losing our middle class and causing growing poverty, widening the gap between the rich and poor to a terrifying amount.

We focus so much on a couple of areas of the problem. Politics or education reform is the principal topic we search for in a solution. These two ideas simply mask the real complication that all politicians and educators are missing. It simply just masks the fact that the rich are getting richer and the poor are getting poorer. It is nothing new, nor is it new that the middle class demand better politicians and a better way of life.

Where we all have been failing, lies in where we search for answers. Through years of distress and numerous "experts" that claim to have found the answer, life never really changes. Lately, it seems to only get worse.

Recently, we have been hearing politicians promising a lot for the middle class on both sides of the political spectrum. The problem, the answer, and the solution all lie in ourselves.

We need our own leaders and our own fact finders. When we rely on others, we can easily be manipulated and be given the wrong answers, sometimes even deliberately.

We often enjoy overthinking and overheating our minds to make life more difficult. Here's your answer. If you want to find an answer or a way out, you must do it yourself. Through much of our own research, we have taken facts and lessons that we have learned along the way of our own journey to find out why the rich get richer and the poor get poorer.

As one of the authors, I will quickly give a feel of some of my personal experiences.

"This all really started growing up as a poor kid with a poor mentality. I knew there had to be a way out, but along the way I discovered being rich was more than just about money. First, I had to learn the hard way that being mentally rich was the first step to take to ever achieve total freedom, happiness, or great wealth."

Materialism from great riches comes from only stuffing the truth down. Many have never become mentally rich at first. Therefore, they have no idea what a life should be. Belongings and possessions take over and what is truly important is forgotten.

This dream life we crave can be attained. It is for everyone and anyone, yet society has put changes on so many. It is far too often that we do not live up to our full potential and lead a life off of our path.

This is so important to consider, especially in modern times. Times have been tough lately, especially financially. We are living in a time where another depression looms.

Entrepreneurship is the only hope for surviving the always changing world. This has always been true, but is becoming much truer today. Let's consider what we are talking about when we speak of another depression looming.

In a later chapter we will discuss this same topic, but in further detail. There are over $1 quadrillion in derivatives floating out there. In 2007, the economy crashed and the United States suffered a recession. There were roughly $700 trillion in derivatives. When these types of derivatives, or "bubbles" (as many are more familiar with), pop they crash the economy and the poor and middle class suffer tremendously while many times the rich richer.

Now let's hope that this never happens. While it is a very serious threat, let's prepare just in case.

CHAPTER 2

TAUGHT TO FAIL

The fear of the future lies in all of us. This is pretty easy to see as society itself is appearing to lose hope.

We have come so far in this country only to rely on others to better themselves. This is most prevalent in searching for the next heroic politician. At the time that we cannot find one, then we search for the perfect school.

Unfortunately, this is only making matters worse as an increased amount of news stories are conducted detailing the drowning student debt that is out there. To be precise, over $1 trillion of it.

Well, what do we expect when the government is just printing money for the schools? Let's also look at what we do not learn in school, such as money.

About half of American colleges will be bankrupt or in serious economic distress in the next two decades. This compelling statement goes hand in hand with another issue. Robots, those dreaded man made creatures composed of metal, could take over 20 million jobs by 2030. Include the fact that the United States added 700,000 millionaires in 2017. This number has been increasing over the last decade.

All of this is fascinating considering the gap between the rich and poor is expanding. However, let's consider for a moment, those in this new rich are taking a different path that the others do not. The new rich that are ending income inequality in their own way, through entrepreneurship and a better financial education.

When you add in all the factors above, we can see where the problem and solution stand.

If we can ever change the world for the better, we must first do that for ourselves. There is a demand for change, and again, it lies in each and every one of us wanting a better life.

The act of bringing out the best in ourselves is very much possible. We must restructure, most wouldn't have a problem accepting this. Often problems arrive when we consider where we restructure. School will only get more expensive while it does not ever teach you how to pay off that extreme and useless debt. As long as we wait for politicians to create better policies to better our lives, they will only get more corrupt. The problems will never get solved because the problem lies in us. We must persist through the worst of times, whether it is our fault or not. We could blame and point fingers, but what both political parties need to know is that we must adjust to the current situation in order to succeed.

There are plenty of examples of great leaders and figures in history that succeeded in the worst times.

There is a universal code and method for success. It does not matter what a country or person has gone through, everyone and anyone can change their life and succeed.

We can better the world only if we perform these actions first. A dream life will not occur before one becomes mentally rich. Just like many tasks in life, there is a process that needs to be performed to get the desired result.

We often hear how people hold us down, we certainly did at one point. For a great part of many people's lives, they are never free. No matter what we experience and handle, no one can truly hold us down. It is only our poor mindsets that stop our freedom.

It is an easy and enlightening experience. Discovering yourself and creating your own path to travel down is rewarding and makes every single day count. It all stems from the very first step taken, just like the hardest step when you first wake up.

You must first learn to know yourself. Considering who you are, where you come from, and how you got here is knowledge that will give you an insight as to how to better your life.

Finding what your strengths and weaknesses are will be your greatest investment and asset you can have. Swallowing any pride and defeating your ego to dig deep down to your greatest fears and weaknesses will transform you into the best version of yourself.

We found from our own experience as to why things in life seem to be so "unfair." In the end, we found that the barriers we faced were actually built by us. This enforces the statement that few of us are actually ourselves. We have spent a lot of time finding ways to get out of our poor mindset to achieve a rich life.

It was then that we started to become interested in why so many are poor, both mentally and financially. Value is so important to a healthy life. While having good values is important, putting value into your life needs to be the second part of your values.

This comes from being free, happy, and lastly rich.

It is becoming the main factor of today's tensions and economic disaster. The 1930s depression has met the 1960s society tensions and this is what we are left with.

If more people valued entrepreneurship and being a strong leader, the gap between the rich and poor can decrease. It is the mindset of this new rich that is ever growing.

CHAPTER 3

MONEY ILLUSION

Money is the main cause of the current massive political divide. In order to avoid a lengthy discussion as to who is to blame, let's just stick to what is most significant.

The only reason for such dire financial times is that money has changed, but understanding of it has not. It is the single biggest reason for poverty.

If you are illiterate, then you cannot read. The same goes for money, if you are illiterate of money, you cannot be rich.

The simple idea of money has become the root of all problems, stemming from the most paramount problem: why the rich are getting richer and the poor are falling deeper into poverty.

When you understand money, you can see that it is worthless. Money has absolutely no value. The hundred dollar bill is just as worthless as the one dollar bill.

To keep the understanding of the topic brief, we will travel to the year of 1971. The United States dollar was taken off of the gold standard. This allowed for the government to print money, also known as Fiat money. Fiat money is fake money because it is solely printed by the government. Without valuing the dollar next to gold, it then becomes worthless.

Misunderstanding of money has caused people to live in chaos. Without populating the country with rich and free people, countries live in poverty until there is a revolution. Luckily the United States experienced this in 1776, so a violent revolt will never need to take place again.

The revolution today is an ethical and financially literate group of people. It is the simple misunderstanding of true financial literacy that caused people to be poor.

The new form of Fiat money that is printed at high levels is simply paper and has zero value. The only possibility that money has any value is if it is being used to make more money. Basically, if your money is not being used to make more, then it is being lost.

To put it simply, value in money is only based on assets. You either have an asset or a liability. Many will see a home as an asset, but since the house takes money out of your account, it is a liability.

Owning rental property makes you money without "working". This places money into your account and is considered an asset.

This is Financial Literacy 101, and yet people are still in disagreement on whether a house is an asset or liability.

Let's think about the gap between the rich and poor. One side struggles and has low financial literacy. The other side is rich and have learned money along with business sense, leading to little financial problems. These are the same people who always seem to survive a rough patch in our society. They always get richer and they never lose anything during a recession.

WHAT UNITES US?

Many cannot agree on a single idea anymore, except for the fact that they are fighting about the same thing. Whether people admit it or not, every reason for difficult times and tensions are due to the constant fact that the rich get richer and the poor get poorer.

People who are the most divided in this country are actually in the same position. Many, although unintentionally, hide behind political affiliations and search for the answer to fix it all.

The same people who hate each other on the political spectrum can actually agree that people are getting richer and others are getting poorer. Sometimes these two factors are not dependent on the other.

Through much research that we have found in the majority of people, we are more connected than we notice. We are all connected, even in the most divided political times. The citizens of the United States of America are getting poorer as the years go by and little hope can be found. The main dilemma lies in the biggest divider, and that's how to solve the problem.

We cannot even come close to solving the major problems that have plagued society from the very beginning (lack of knowledge in the self and money) without first starting at the absolute smallest step there is. It first lies deep in the heart of every individual. Deeper than our identity or social belonging, we are all individuals and what eventually connects us is our desire to identify.

Possessing a care and love for your culture, heritage, and religion is crucial to a healthy life. Try and think even deeper. Pull up what lies at the very heart of what makes you happy and different from everybody else. Perhaps that realization will help you to notice the passion that you have, ultimately leading to a happy, free life with a rich mindset and rich life.

Change is a difficult and laborious subject for a large number of us. A slight change in routine or familiar presence is all it takes for one to feel high stress levels.

For us, we had trouble doing this as well as others did. The ability to admit your failures are caused by us and our poor mindsets can whip some people into insanity.

The hopeful and enlightening take is that it does not have to be a painful transition. In fact, it makes every day count more as each day passes. Knowing your strengths allow our self-confidence to grow.

It lies in our weaknesses that cause people to start disliking themselves. Being able to face your fears and admit there must be a change is strong and courageous. It is in our mindsets where we do not see that and we start to blame others for where we are. As humans, we are eager to blame others for an unwanted event occurring. Begin to think of how we can avoid problems and make situations more desirable.

Something made us think about our future and where life was truly headed. We weren't content. We already weren't joyous with the path that we were traveling down. We knew a change had to be made immediately.

We reached this point in our life by truly finding ourselves and, in the process, realized we found it through the goodness of others. We broke from our ego and old failing mindset. We knew that we had to be honest with ourselves, but as we did this, we later came to see very few do it.

This is not preaching ourselves and giving us a pat on the back, but rather as a chance to see life differently. We wish for all people to be empowered enough to see that in the end all they need to do is chase what makes them free, happy and rich, both mentally and financially.

We were tired of constantly failing and not being truly happy in life. Deep down, we knew this would never make us rich in life. When it came to viewing our future as a miserable, we knew a massive change was needed.

"I made a giant change in deciding that I would reach my highest potential. I had been through so much in my life. I came to see the events that plagued my life actually made me stronger. I noticed that I did not care as much about what others thought and focused only on what I thought. We all try to train ourselves to truly believe that and believe me, it is not easy. Often this leads to people walking around with a fake smile. Deep down the pain is there and then you continue to lose faith. I know this because I have been there many times. You must be honest with yourself in order for life to world in your favor. You cannot fake happiness. Eventually it will destroy you more than anyone ever could. The real reason for our unhappiness is the thing that gets stuffed down the most. It is our biggest insecurity. This arises from our past that we have not yet let go of. In order to ever live in the present and look forward to the future, you must let go of the past. Every life is its only story. Your life book has a beginning, middle, and end. There are good chapters and bad chapters. What is different about life is that every chapter can be better than the last. An author controls their own book's plot, but being the author of your own life will allow for continuous excitement."

You have total creative control of your own life whether one can see that or not. The truly free, happy, and rich people have discovered this "secret."

This simple mindset change is all that separates the successful from the unsuccessful, the happy from the sad, and the free from the imprisoned life. All we care about is taking you down a path where you have all the freedom, happiness, and riches that you have ever wanted. This is your path.

Many of you are not journeying down your path. You have the tools and are smarter than you think, and are probably even smarter than us. Live the life you have always wanted because you finally deserve it.

MIND YOUR BUSINESS

If you've ever had that one very notable action that you've always wanted to do, the thing that you say you would drop everything to pursue, then it is time to take that move.

We had to fail a million times in order to finally find ourselves and figure out what would make us successful.

Many end up getting held back from that jump due to it being hard to know where to start. It is difficult to be motivated and succeed when you have not found what your purpose is. "I was stuck at this point in my life and was afraid I would be stuck for many years. I did not want to sacrifice my freedom and happiness for the rest of my life. I knew it was time for this change. I just decided to look within myself and pull out all that held me down. I finally accepted my past as my part of my story. I was now willing to change because I accepted I needed a change. This takes being brutally honest with yourself."

Once you let go of the past, you can live in the moment. Time feels real and you see the light in life. Dark days make for an even lighter day. This is how we truly become present. It awakens a side of you that is more creative and positive than you realized you were capable of. This awakens the realization that you are in total control. A realization that few see is that living for the thrill is living in the present.

You have discovered the secret to being fully free and happy in your own life through your own power. This really is the first step in a better life. If you cannot be happy and free from within, you will always rely on others.

This is most prominent in terms of money. The number is far too low for those that are creating their own income. There is a huge demand for entrepreneurs, but people continue to become employees. The real reason for the pains of globalization is that there is not enough of us taking advantage of new technologies and new ways to make money on our own.

Are we saying that being an employee is bad? Of course not. Every profession is just as important as any, but there is a low demand for more employees within that profession. Take teachers for instance. We need teachers and value them as well, but it almost appears as if that is not the case. Even colleges are not viewed as important as they once were. With the rise of tuition that leads to student debt, a lot of hopeful students are determining it is not worth it.

Again, there is a low demand for another college graduate that wants to become another employee. We need to learn from the entrepreneurs rather than the teachers. The greatest opportunity arises in the difficulty itself. We require more scientists and teachers becoming entrepreneurs and solving problems within their profession for the advancement of society.

Formal education is vital, but it cannot be your only education. Attending college does not have to be a waste of time. Once you receive your formal education, it is balancing your non-formal education that leads to success.

There is a whole list of ideas that you will never be taught in school. This is not an excuse to disagree with school. That is our job. Education has become an institution to put you down the path that all travel.

Everyone individual faces obstacles and these barriers they face often keep them pressed down the entirety of their lives. It becomes their identity and their excuse. Most fail to see that this is hardly ever our fault. Attaching to the past only prevents you from moving on. Moving on is the first step in starting your "new" life.

Of course, a non-formal education has to start somewhere. The first thing to do after starting over is to acquire a plan.

"Instead of a goal, I stick to a set of rules or a guide to follow. I follow what makes me free, happy, and rich, both mentally and financially."

Once you follow this system, and have succeeded, the next phase should be to pass these tools to others. It is not an idea to preach. You are just bringing out another person's true inner self. We are capable of more than we realize. The process of getting people to see just how much control they have over their own life is not as impossible as it is made to be. We must see that all have potential in this life. Someone who fails, at any time in their lives, whether they be young or old, can always start over and try again. Age is but a number, take a look at the ages of the founders of McDonald's and Kentucky Fried Chicken.

Failing is a part of life. The only true failure is giving up and accepting defeat. It has been said for years, but it is easier said than done. Our minds accept defeat way too soon due to their deep down fears. Staying present brings an awareness to get back on your feet and try again.

The underlying reason people fail at their dreams, or never even pursue them, is because they never create a plan. This is not a business plan, but rather a life plan. Seeing a life in which you have total control allows you to create a system and plan for staying in control. The mind remains active and always motivated. Discover what you need to succeed and learn the system as you go. The result will be successfully walking down your own path. Few are ever taught this as many depend solely on a formal education. Therefore, numerous people never create their own plan and end up lost many years later.

This is the only plan you will ever need. Not only are you going solely down your own path, but you are training yourself to never let yourself fail. You are programmed to never give up. Rather than just saying it and having a backup plan, you will never accept failure. You keep persisting until you have reached the finish line.

Those that finally make their jump, often fail too soon. By fail, we mean give up. Importance of failing is frequently missed, no exception to us. Failing is the greatest lesson you will ever learn. That is, if you choose to view it this way. For some, they fail and give up. Learning from the mistakes and trying again is an almost guaranteed way to ever succeed in the long run.

We knew that our lives had several failures. Many of us fail too often when we dig deep at the root of who we are. We let it define us to the point that we believe we have failed. These are the steps that teach you to let go of the past. See and try new experiences while also embracing failure as a way to grow and become a better version of yourself.

"I was going through the motions. I could tell I was just drifting through life, waiting for an opening to be presented to me. Over time, with this new self-reflection that we have talked about so far, I finally saw what I wanted in life and I was not going to let anyone get in my way. Even I was not going to even think about failing. I was genuinely convinced I could do it and when I was locked and loaded, I was ready for the beginning of the rest of my life. Part 2 of my life was just beginning. I was anticipated and motivated. I felt like I was in the fast lane of my own path. What truly prepared me for this jump, was understanding that it has to be done in slow steps. Being at the bottom of my plan A sure felt better than getting ready for a 9-5 job after I graduated college. I was content with that, and therefore, knew I could achieve it. Part 2 of your life is finally being on your own path and in your plan A. this part requires so many more risks than you have ever experienced. You need to be totally focused 100% of the time. Every day is a new day and new lessons are to be learned throughout this time. Always prepare for your future self. Eventually you will be put into a situation where your jump has finally paid off. Until that happens, treat every situation as if it is a practice test."

CHAPTER 4

GET BACK UP

It is imperative to act on the enlightened ideas that you own. There is nothing wrong with dropping it all to better yourself. Emerge as a new person that people do not recognize.

Display to others how happy you are. The world you create can inspire others. The sole reason for this is to better the world.

As we transform our lives, we learn along the way in order to defeat fear. This results in the courage to be your new and real self. All great leaders are created in this system. Do not be afraid to get back up while you are knocked down. Come back stronger than ever and let go of the past.

We must always control our happiness and emotions, even in a time of attack on our mental state. The hate you keep inside is much more damaging than the attack you face.

We have all been knocked down at least once in our lives. It might have been something small that got to us, or a major life-altering scenario. It is easy to urge others to get back up, but in reality, getting knocked down too many times can leave you thinking it is where you belong.

The people who get knocked down the most, or fail the most, have the most potential. Few too many choose the more rigorous path because of the extreme risk. The more you fail, the more risk you have taken. Every failure puts you one step closer to your goals.

It is often why many who rarely fail and get sucked in the pits of the 9-5 life often never are truly happy, even after they have climbed the ranks to a six-figure salary. Although there is not as much risk in this path, it does not mean the 9-5 option is inferior.

We are talking about the risky jump and the safety path of life. The safer 9-5 path can deliver plenty of happiness, but to truly achieve all the more freedoms and financial freedoms, plenty of risk needs to be taken. During such dire financial times, the most financially independent people survive. With the proper financial education, you could walk out of a recession with a huge profit.

While money and the process of acquiring it has changed, so should the knowledge of it. Most people are victims of a lack of knowledge of money. While so many are struggling these days, financial dependence will be crucial for survival. Of course, this will never happen until we take care of ourselves and live a full life. In the end, the sacrifices you take only lead to a more successful life. Never be afraid to fail.

The further you fail, the closer you get to that dream destination. The first failure often leads people to give up immediately and take the safe path. While this may be the right choice for some, the rest end up unhappy with a lack of freedom down the road. It ultimately leads people to life's greatest dilemma, whether making a jump is even worth it at all.

Taking the jump is a certain occurrence once you put your all into it. Everything that makes you who you are needs to go into this jump. People who take this risk either succeed big or fall hard. You only lose if you fail, and you only fail when you give up. Keep going. What is on the other side is worth this life changing jump to your dream life.

It is effortless to consider someone's success and think how "lucky" they are.

"For myself, I did not think just anyone could accomplish their goals. A dream life did not seem like a chance."

"It was my lack of mental freedom that stopped my financial freedom. Before I ever realized what had to come first in life, I was lost. Very few people see the possibilities in life. As I started to believe in myself, I knew I actually had no idea where to go. I started to notice scarcely any of us are own our own path."

"I knew it would be hard while being full of doubt and failures, but I knew it would be worth it. To express this idea of mental and financial freedom, I knew that I had to reach a great many people."

"The reason being, I knew people have the potential to better their lives. Restoring hope requires a lot of action. We weren't going into this expecting anything to go our way. We knew that there would be failures and an abundance of obstacles along the way. Rather than letting this become our identity, it allowed us to face life head on with little to no fear."

If you challenge the status quo, you will never receive encouragement at first. The road less traveled is not often thought of as a first option.

Hence, when you find your own road and stop following everyone else, they question. This rarely comes from a place of anger. People have been trained to not think for their individual selves for a large portion of their life. Whether this falls on parents or the education system is a debate for another time.

To have a self-education is to be solely responsible for the way your life turns out. Others cannot be blamed if you are not free, happy, or rich in your own life. This idea is not even considered anymore. The ways to success that Abraham Lincoln and Albert Einstein used were the most successful methods.

The method of self-education is a major investment that leads to the phrase we use known as "self-rich". Self-education can be synonymous with self-made. We prefer the term rich instead of made because we learn from so many people. All of us are made through others and their rich ideas and actions.

So many great independent thinkers like Thomas Edison and Nikola Tesla taught us more than anyone else has. What they have accomplished could not have been possible without their given mindset. Combined with his inventions, Edison had the business sense to maximize his success in other areas of his life. The wealth that one makes hails nothing in comparison to the contributions you make. Money means nothing if it provides no value.

The act of being rich consists of more than just the money that we have. Rich implies that you are rich mentally, as well as financially. Self-education teaches just how to better your own life, mentally and financially.

This procedure takes an incredible amount of persistence. Each person is capable of persevering through anything that is thrown at them. Learn from past mistakes to live today and plan for the future you want.

"I had failed so many times in my life. Eventually, I decided to give up on dreams and just find a good job once I graduated college. Safety and security always seemed to sound like a reasonable choice."

"I researched many jobs trying to fit their qualifications. Mainly, I was searching for a job that would make my life better. I was not looking for the best job, but rather the job that wouldn't put me to sleep. This was ultimately when the voice deep down inside said that this is not what life was meant to be. I had been through too much in life to ever settle."

Schools are failing the youth and we are not going to ignore this fact. You may never learn about how to make money, or even have a better understanding of how money works. While considering employment or simple daily tasks, occupying a sense of money and how it works is key to success.

It gets worse. We are never taught about ourselves. When we have let go of the past and are ready for a better life, it is hard to know where to start. The biggest reason we do not make our leap is the fear of failing. We fear failure because we are taught that failing is wrong. Without failure, there is no success. To never fail, is to never reach your full potential.

Without limits, without the fear of failure, the world becomes yours. We become enlightened when we only see the positive and hopeful side to life.

It is in this current state of life where you are most calm. Every day has new meaning, the current state is peaceful, the past is gone, and the future seems even better than today is.

It is the dream life that we search for, yet never find. We searched high and low before we noticed the answer was ourselves. Mindsets are built by us, so it is up to us to be the creator of it.

When you only look at the future and have no holds on the past, it is easier to no longer dread failure.

The exceptional quote from FDR, "the only thing we have to fear is fear itself" needs a slight change for today's world. The only thing we have to fear is failure seems a bit clearer. Fear needs a new meaning. Avoiding the actions in which you "fear" only makes them worse. We can conquer fear by living in a more present state. It is only then that we can embrace "failure." In order for success to happen, we must be willing to fail.

Failing is simply just a lesson is disguise. For the time being, let's look at "fearing failure" as a way to defeat it. Fear failure not because you think it is possible, but rather fear failure because it is simply something you cannot, or will not, accept.

Fearing failure allows you to possess better self-awareness to see where you are failing. Fear failing and you can easily defeat your fears. It is no longer enough to say face your fears. Do not face them, defeat them.

A fighter does not go into a bout with the thought of "I need to get out of this alive." Rather, they admit that they need to beat the opponent, no matter the cost is to them. Each person has a fight that they had or will have to fight. We rarely ever go into a battle by choice. For some, especially when they have poor mental or financial situations, they may avoid their fight and accept the failure they had faced. That failure should have been a lesson that brought out a powerful fighter within yourself.

Instead, a lot of us, including ourselves at one point, take every little thing personally. Our assignment is to keep ourselves happy, even in the worst of times. No one can escape a wall in their road. Accept that things just happen in life. While we cannot control situations and events, we can control our opportunities for a better outcome.

By fearing failure, we make the decision to avoid it completely. Avoiding failure by giving into fears only takes you down a safe and secure road. When making major life decisions, we seldom center our attention on our own well-being first. The average person will think of every excuse in the book to never make their jump.

Accept that life has its bad days. Until you fail, you will never succeed. If your current life is not what it should be, maybe a simple mindset change could turn it all around. There are truly endless opportunities out there. As technology becomes more advanced, earning money is as easy as working from home, without a boss. While we live in a society with the easiest and most opportunistic chances for being an entrepreneur, people still choose the safe and secure "job" route.

Your jump needs to have a passion and work ethic that you, and only you, have full control of. It must be everything you are and stand for. While money is crucial, your values and passions are your greatest reason for working on your grind.

You must have a 50/50 balance of today and the future. Live today, no matter how hard or hopeless, to better tomorrow. Do not miss out on today just to prepare for tomorrow, and do not live today as if you are invincible to the future. This view sounds perfect, as many live by such memorable quotes. Do not forget about taking actions and performing minor actions to succeed in your new enlightened state.

This will result in more clarity throughout a given day and adds meaning to each one. Objects may stand out that you once did not notice. To us, this is the best reason for making every day count. The quote that typically stands out is "live everyday like it's your last."

This does not instruct you to be so carefree as to have absolutely no direction or purpose. Rather, prepare for a life that can be labeled as a happy one. For those with a big dream, or a life that is everything you have ever wanted but with the pieces not quite there yet,

consider this question. If you were to leave a legacy

behind, what would that legacy look like?

CHAPTER 5

<u>YOUR LEGACY</u>

"My main reason for making my jump was knowing I had nothing to lose. We all deserve the life we desire. We owe it to ourselves to delve into the unknown and see what's on the other side."

Once you are capable of accepting this reality, knowing where to start is often what creates the biggest barrier to face. Take into consideration that small, gradual steps need to be taken.

We do not jump head-first into the shallow end of a pool. It is only going to result in disaster. Failing does not have to be this all powerful and consuming thing. Small steps only have small failures. Eventually, failing becomes necessary to keep building your path. Many fail hard because they never built their path's foundation.

A failure that shakes your world is a great fear but it does not have to be. The concept of time and age needs to be let go, along with the past. Growing up is all about numbers, whether that is graduation from higher education, a "big" job, or settling down. This is not for everyone. If life is more focused on quantity instead of quality, then you are never present and free from that stress.

We set goals within a specific time. Frequently, we are told that those around us want to graduate by a certain age, be married within a set of years, or the worst one yet, "I'll follow my own path until I hit this age, then it's back to the safe and secure path." This thinking will never allow you to be present.

"For much of my life, I was guided on achieving the next task to get to the perfect job. This life is now the norm. What I thought was a proper education, would actually result in more and more student debt. Perhaps, it is in our schools that we are the most misguided. For the sake of the argument, it is important to know that just having a formal education cannot achieve entrepreneurial success."

Self-knowledge takes much effort to pursue. The ability to maintain a will to learn and succeed outside of the classroom is what truly creates a rich person.

The rationale behind many rich entrepreneurs not possessing a college degree is that they see where they need to be present at. Some even avoid college altogether. This is not to disparage the education system. It is a reminder that what we need to be taught to succeed, is not found there at traditional colleges.

With the rising student debt, some even feel it is unnecessary altogether. Clearly, a much smaller business loan has a better return than student loans.

A notification popped up on the computer on a Sunday afternoon that read "34 days unemployed, it's getting easier for me to start a company than it is to get a job." This notification from Reddit speaks true to the America that we are living in now.

There is a demand for new business and ideas. Our current system and mindset tells us to go be another employee. While being an employee is not awful, there is not as much demand for them like there once was previously.

A fresh and new wave of entrepreneurs is the new demand. There are very few that have ever even used that word (entrepreneur). Entrepreneurs have always been existent in our society. The ratio of entrepreneurs to employees was monumental.

With all of the changes to American society, from the way money has been devalued to artificial intelligence (AI) and other technologies, it is much easier to become an entrepreneur. Creating your own income has never been quite so easy. Perhaps at one point, someone dreamed of a world in which we are all creating our own independent wealth in a free society. If there ever was a time when we needed more business and wealth, it is now in the present. The only way to end the income gap is through entrepreneurship.

This is especially clear with globalization and artificial intelligence. As many are familiar with manufacturing jobs being outsourced or replaced with robots, white collar jobs are now joining in. With many jobs being replaced with AI and colleges going broke, it seems like taking the entrepreneurial route makes the most sense.

Of course, this idea must challenge every major opinion out there. That's what change does. If we are not willing to accept change and the potential it has, we will remain poor, both mentally and financially.

"It was all a massive confusion to me, as it is when you first discover the truth. So much of what we were used to was changing. I am seeing more and more young people feel hopeless that much of the older generations feel. Things should not be that way."

"It is why we need less formal schooling and more of a non-formal/self-education. I came to see this when I realized that I did not know what I called my passion or what my dream life should look like. It is often so hard to finally put yourself first."

When you take control, being your own leader, or CEO as you will read about later, is a massive responsibility. In one way or another, a "better" education needs to be replaced with the proper education.

Education is, and always will be, the key to a more preferable life and a life that satisfies you. The right education will change your life and bring you out of the worst times. A narrow view of what an education really is became the norm.

Possessing an education is confused with being educated. The majority of young people are now taught to acquire great debt before the age of 21, just to have a job. The younger years of our lives should be spent making mistakes and learning from them. There is no such thing as failing when you are young. From a very early age, failure is frowned upon, and that rarely changes for students all the way through college.

Education first starts with the self. Learning and growing cannot happen with a lack of understanding of who you are in your current state. There is never stress or fear in our current state. For a life filled with hardship, why not prepare?

A particular area of schooling that we have failed is our fascination on numbers and our focus on the quantity rather than the quality. This has been programmed into us from a young age. You cannot set goals based on a silly timeframe. You will end up in school for an "X" number of years or be at a certain job for so long. You were just living to get by before you left this world. You were dying for the next thing, and all the while you forgot to live.

This is the reality for a good portion of people. Many do not notice it until it is truly too late. They do not truly understand that this life only happens once and is so temporary. When you accept this simple truth, you have freed yourself of everyone else's path. Your life is your life. Plain and simple. Why not make the most of it?

It's not easy for us to understand the reasons that we have many time frames set up for life. Society has taken these people from their own path and put them on the "normal one." This is very prevalent in this state of the world. We have feared failure so much that we totally avoid it and become sheltered from the world.

These ideas are what keeps people locked down. They are setting goals for themselves that will satisfy society and their rules.

Of course, this has been a long and calm removal of who we are. We often become so blind to this that they will step on other's dreams and even laugh at how "late" they take their jump. Some will even laugh at another person's jump altogether. They see your jump as a failure because it is what society taught them it is. Life becomes nothing but a race. This is where people confuse quality with quantity.

This results in very little effort being put into their life. A life that is treated as a race instead of a marathon cannot be lived to its fullest potential.

Finally seeing this is freeing. You know it does not come from a place of hate. Rather, deep down they see you breaking free of those chains. There is nothing faulty with a job and paying bills. Creating a family is a grateful experience. This is what is truly important in life. However, there needs to be more quality to that life that you create.

The most important thing overlooked is ourselves. We try to help others before we consider helping ourselves. We cannot change the world until we change ourselves. Even those who see this truth too late are never too late to still make their jump.

"Had more of us have been educated in this, myself included, then we could have prevented the problems facing many today. This took me years to see this. Schooling and especially college, are crucial to our country's advancement. In fact, education reform would change the entire world and bring world peace. What we need to reform first, is what is being taught."

Embracing failure can open up a new way you view the world. Accepting that failure will happen and being prepared will eliminate the stress that you will have. Remember to embrace the journey, no matter how vigorous it might be. The best way to enjoy your life's destination, is to embrace the journey along the way.

Perhaps you think you have failed, but you know now that failing is only true when you have accepted it. With this new realization, you can break from society's standards and can now focus on your own.

Remember that life is only temporary. We are not entitled to a long life, but we are entitled to a great life, however long that may be. When this reality sets in, it will be a stage in your life where you need to take advantage of the fact that this is all temporary. Be truly present.

Letting go of the past gives you the freedom to move on. Our first introduction of freedom in life should first start with our own search for it. Problems will arise, that is inevitable in life. What we take away from such an event is up to us.

Learning from your past mistakes can guide you to a better future. It is this understanding of life that allows you to only be forced into the present. It is the least painful and liberated place one can possibly be in. Being present and at peace will clear the road in your path to riches. This is where you will see more opportunities when life gets worse and worse, whether that be in the world or even in yourself. A brighter way of seeing and analyzing problems rather than shying away and criticizing them is what separates the happy from those who cannot create that happiness.

Keep in mind that you control the quality of your own life and you can see that the little things in life do not matter.

The unchallenging piece is realizing that you control the quality. The hard part is accepting that you do not have control over the quantity.

"When I came to see this and embrace this simple truth, I felt freedom like I had never felt before."

Worrying about the most miniscule things will tire you out. It will consume the time you have and leave little for pursuing dreams and personal goals. There are many times throughout a day that will consume your time when it can easily be ignored. Imagine how much more time you could see that you have when you cut out all of the distractions.

CHAPTER 6

GET STARTED

Most of us strive for a life in which we are free, happy, and rich. Of course, this is only obtained through ourselves. It is easier to accomplish your dreams with this revelation. When we boil down what life is, we determine that it is living a lifestyle that really suits you. Find your purpose. What will you leave behind that makes you unique and different from the norm?

In taking the leap to your dream lifestyle, you can start taking steps right as you read it. What is the absolute first step in reaching your dream? Take small steps today. Ignoring a time frame will free up your time to do whatever it takes and powers you through, no matter how long, until your dreams are reached. Just know that one day you will get there. Remember failure is only a choice. Only we are our barriers. Take your time and have a system.

"I find that having a system to constantly grow helps to make every day count."

"I am not concerned with a plan because it is a little too formal for me. For me, it creates that timeframe that takes away the quality of life. You will become lost in numbers. The need to achieve goals at a young age, to have the money and status that comes with it, is built from having a plan."

A system allows for life to act in its current, present state. This allows for you to easily balance your time as you now see you had more time than you really thought. Your distractions will be erased, along with the negative energy.

Do not just live for the weekend. If your life has become that, perhaps it is time for a change. Counting down the days just to finally do what you want, just to go back to work in two days, is a dead-end. Of course, this sounds easier said than done. First, know that there is no age limit or requirement for actually living a fulfilling life.

There is a will to grow, learn, and create your own lifestyle that makes you happy, free, and rich. It takes a lengthy amount of time to ever find yourself and what your true passions are.

For some, they never find it, and there is that deep down feeling of regret and what ifs. The problem people do not see, is that there is no rule book. Keep in mind that every decision you make affects your own life. Not one person can truly create their own destination. Problems can occur that you do not control. Although, you can see that it falls on you to make it out. This is an age old fact that has been buried for too long. Personally, it is the result of a broken person that has led to a broken world. Just as one idea can change the world, one negative emotion can spread like a disease and affect a mass of people. The way to get back on the right path, is to get on our own individual path.

In order to succeed and change the world, small steps must be taken to make the world a better place, and to make yourself better as well. Every single day must be better than the last. It begins with making small steps to better your own day. Your day should be filled with progress in making your dreams happen. Progress often feels like it is lagging along, while in reality, it is for the better. Time and effort must not be taken for granted. Any time you get to work on your grind, that time should be taken and used to its full potential.

Remember, it is not always the time you have, but rather what you put into those limited hours you have. There are plenty of examples of great people who used their time wisely to achieve their goals. Often, we make excuses that we do not have time.

"When I replaced mindless distractions during my leisure time, I noticed a huge change in myself. For one, using free time to advance your goals is part of that slow progress. Those small steps lead up to a big jump into your dream life. Spending time reading outside of a classroom is the greatest form of education."

It is in what we read that makes us who we are. The things we can learn from others keeps us grounded and humble. Our ego is gone as we let others' ideas form our open-minded selves.

"Biographies are the greatest way to learn true success. I grew fascinated with the success stories out there. I found out that the road to their success was just as wonderful as the success they actually had. I saw struggles more than the average person faced, and I saw how they became successful in the end."

"I felt very related to the hard fought battles in those stories, as theirs compared to my own. What I needed, and it seems what many others need as well, was the perseverance and leadership they display. Every successful person had something in common. They were never giving up. This has to be one of the most cliché sayings, but it remains true even in these confusing times."

"As I read more and more successful individual's biographies, I realized that many had the same experiences that I had. I knew their story and how they got to the place they were at. This goes way beyond fame and fortune. Any success story teaches a lesson through the person's failures in life. I had always believed we struggle so hard in life for a bigger reason. Whatever one believes in life, from their religion to their identities, we understand that we have a momentous purpose. Our barriers must be knocked down, from what holds us down mentally and financially."

"I didn't look at my life with pity. I looked at it and thought, "this will make me stronger and ready for whatever life throws at me." As mentioned before, to never have struggle is to never be set up for a great life. If you haven't faced a lot of struggles and haven't fell a lot, then you should start failing more and more."

That may go against everything that you believe in. However, if you ask any successful entrepreneur what it takes, they will say the same statement. Many lose true knowledge and even worse, some are never even taught it. It is why we see so much turmoil in our society. The single greatest problem facing today's citizens is a mentally and financially poor society. The only way to make an authentic positive change is to focus on many of the individual free, happy, and rich. Again, this is where the demand for change lies in the demand for a better self. Your passions and self-rich education can change your life more than any policy or school could.

Ambition should only grow as you do. Ambition and passions do not go away when you finish school. You grow up with continuous ambition. This ambition turns into hunger. For many, ambition that was there at a younger age disappears. Those that retain the hunger and desire to reach their dreams, truly do.

To refer back to our obsession with time instead of quality, our simple understanding of time can open up a new way of thinking. While we are not attempting to go on a spiritual speech, time is essentially an illusion. Time is a major concept that unites every single person. We all have the same amount, from the rich to the poor.

It is imperative to disregard what anyone thinks of you. Do not let it be a reason to give up. Numerous success stories feature people at their very lowest, whether it be their mental or financial state. In the end, you will see that it was you all along that had the power to your own happiness and freedom. You do not want to realize this too late. You have only failed when you stop trying.

It is a realization that many people have it much easier in life than others. Everybody does not have the same fortunes or setbacks. This is a given whether people admit it or not. Privilege is real. Some people have doors already open for them.

For those who have the door shut in their face or have locks on them, bust through. Do not ever wait for someone to open the door for you, whether the door is shut or even locked. Remember that it is your struggle, so get through to the other side.

Accept that you have just as much time as anyone else. It is not an option to think "If there was more time, we could have accomplished so much more." This is never the case. There is always time and this is what separates those that are successful from those that are not.

Sometimes, we need to be a little hard on ourselves. We need to constantly remind ourselves that we have the time for ourselves. Do not let any excuse or limited resources hold you back. Release yourself from the idea that you are a victim of someone else's choices. This is a fact of life, but is it almost impossible to live in a world of zero conflict or problems. There will always be a battle, and regardless of who is to blame, we need to be the ones to make it better. Do not let anyone else's advantage or life keep you from achieving your goals.

Every idea and business could have been thought of by anyone else. It all comes down to who arrives to it first. Invest in yourself so that the only person you will ever rely on is the one in the mirror looking back at you.

The way you feel toward yourself is how you will feel toward others. The fact remains that you cannot change the world until you have changed yourself. You may not have the life that you have always dreamed of at the moment, but that does not mean you have to be unhappy or poor. Think of yourself as a happy person with a broad outlook on life. By telling yourself that you are happy and that life is good, you are at first only convincing yourself.

"I often tried to view life in the same way, but in reality, it was only words and not an actual feeling I had experienced. Many put on a fake smile to convince the world they are happy. Yet, deep down they are truly broken. This is not an easy feat to come out of."

Rather than saying you are happy and faking that smile, approach life with the mindset of a student. We are not meaning a high school or college student. Be a student of life.

Do it for yourself. Learn about the world for your own health. Understanding the world and the reasons behind it.

You have a purpose and you are entitled to make your jump. If you start with one step today, that one step will grow into a journey. Before you are aware of it, you will be down your own path. You will be living the free and happy life that is so heavily mentioned.

PART II:

WHAT IT MEANS TO BE RICH

CHAPTER 7

VISION YOUR FUTURE

"In early 2019, I told myself that I would make the next decade, the 2020s, my time. Once I was able to see this new life that I always had, I knew I had to make the most of it. In the summer of 2019, I decided to make my jump. We decided to write this very book."

"The rest is history. We were just people who had no fear, no money, and no idea where our lives were going."

There were a few things that we did have. It was the freedom to be ourselves. We did not know where our path was yet headed, but we were content with being on our path.

We stuck to the system we had orchestrated of searching for the next thing to help us grow. It was effortless to feel the lift of the world gone from us. The world may be a big and frightening place, but traveling down your own road makes it seem much smaller than it is. This feeling gives the confidence to try anything, even if it means failing.

It is the moment. Finally, that you achieve freedom. This is not the type of freedom many experience.

True freedom is knowing that the only thing that stops you from your dreams and the success that it brings, is you. No one can hold you back.

You must be focusing on yourself and how to better your own life. Therefore, you must realize that, at times, not one person will believe in your dreams. This is crucial to the success entrepreneurs achieve.

In the beginning, do not expect permission. Do not seek support. The very idea of this is to train yourself to only see yourself as the sole provider. You provide your own happiness, freedoms, and income.

You can be held down for so long by the idea that others are the reason for your roadblocks, and that means you are not free. You are only not free from yourself to let go of this idea.

Accept who you are and who you want to be. Traveling down your own road means to no longer be phased by any negativity. Accept that the road less traveled is a bumpy and lonely road at times.

When we took our jump, it made us feel that we were not living by normal circumstances. Viewing the world differently, especially a world where the future has more potential than one believes, is by no means normal. Society has always been trigger-happy to turn an eye to revolutionary ideas. This cannot happen without a proper amount of self-education.

It is the most prepared and safest way of thinking you can have. Perhaps many do not take this road because of fear, but any chance you have to grow, you should take.

Embracing struggle is to lose all fear in the unknowing or in the inevitable. Be prepared for barriers and signs. Struggle in danger.

Let's have a thought break. Picture yourself driving. If you see a caution ahead sign, do you turn around and drive away, or do you buckle up and embrace whatever comes down the road? Fuel yourself with the obsession of the unknown.

There is no such thing as positivity without negativity. There is no rich without poor. Mentioning that situations do not go the way you want in your life is admitting to living in negativity. With your simple mindset change, it is easy to deflect negativity. One cannot control negative situations. What can we do? We can control whether we absorb that negativity or not.

The energy you absorb from other negative people travels from one person to another. Stick to what is positive and has a lesson to learn. Opportunities lie anywhere and everywhere. If you devise a plan to only find a positive outcome, not only does it make you mentally rich, but it can potentially lead to financial richness.

Living your life with a plan sounds as if life is nothing but business. While this may not be a bad thing, it is also not even true. Have a system to get what you need done accomplished. Build a life worth living for tomorrow, but do not forget about the fun and the beauty of just one day. One day can be filled with progress for your growth, but imagine how great the reward will be.

Being in complete control over your own lifestyle is very rare. For those that take the entrepreneurial life, this is the first step in their journey to riches. It comes from having the rich mentality that makes being financially rich much better.

A new wave of independent thinkers must first come from a new wave of people wanting to actually learn. Do not fear change, but most importantly, embrace anything that can potentially better your mental and financial state.

We get lost in own set opinions. This is becoming increasingly easy to see in those that are younger. Many are struggling to find hope in their own futures, so they have already given up on the world. Do whatever it takes to succeed, embrace all and any ideas.

Frequently, when we consider giving up, an opportunity arises. Until that lucky break happens, begin each day by preparing for the moment that it happens.

It has become increasingly difficult to fix the mental and financial problems of today. The simple loss of freedom and independence can lead to a natural disaster that has taken decades to fix.

The art of being guided by someone else in your own path will lead you to a place you were never meant to be. An overwhelming amount of time in our lives is spent following others and relying on their happiness to have our own. This was never in the plan of our unique life, yet here we are.

Entrepreneurs are more likely to have greater freedom and happiness. Again, while working for someone is honorable and indeed necessary to our society, it is not for everyone. For some, working for others can make them question who they are and the worth that life has. Stuffing these thoughts deeper leads to the mind weakening and distracts us from the point of life.

Passions cannot be pushed aside for anything or anyone. As we get older and compromise our lives, the only one to suffer is the self. How does one explain the anger that so many feel? The result is from a prolonged time of being led down a road that wasn't created for them, passions becoming the past, and the self getting more and more off-track.

It is who we have become. It is seen every day in our world. Anger, hate, and unhappiness stem from our path being abandoned for the wrong one. The helpless, lost feeling that so many experience is not quite the feeling it is. We are never lost, only misguided.

Take a peek at the political divide. Essentially, it originated from a lack of identity in individuals. This is the poor mental attitude that hurts us which leads to our poor financial state, as seen in the dangers of income inequality.

The wrong path has led us down a dark and eerie trail with no identity, resulting in hate, frustration and division. We have become grouped into two possible members of society. Individuality is shrinking due to ongoing social norms that take you off of your path. Being misguided for so long is causing many to feel as if they are lost with no chance of ever being found. This is a representation of what society is as a whole. A hopeless, misguided soul is one that will never achieve a happy life, or great riches.

Self-love is the first step of obtaining freedom. It is how we initiate finding what makes a person who they are. Without that freedom, one is no longer a whole, but rather a part of a larger structure. They are warped into believing whatever the norm is before the self ever sees it through. The self gets ignored and the reaction is filled with hate and anger.

CHAPTER 8

WHAT DO YOU WANT TO BE WHEN YOU GROW UP?

"There was never a time for us to actually know what we wanted to do with our lives. Our passion was being carefree. From a young child, I had chased many dreams with big payoffs. While I had failed many times, it was when I grew older that I realized I had entrepreneurial traits. Have you ever failed at a task after trying and somebody laughed at your or your effort? If so, you may be on the right track."

The idea of being in the norm was never satisfying enough. We sought a world that was simple, free, and rich. We are told to reach for the sky, but only for so long. Folks expect that this lifestyle will fade, along with the school bus that no longer picks you up. There seems to be a system where a collective group live. It begins with our time after graduating high school. After required schooling is completed, many are told to grow up and find a safe job, or a "normal" life. The "real world" needs to be the only path that one is permitted to take.

In the "real world", there are demands that we have never been prepared for. Money and understanding of how it works is never even taught to anyone. The hardest lessons we ever learn in life are those that we are never ready for. The method to live a life is comprised for safety and security. The golden years of our lives need to be used to try, fail, and grow. That freedom has been taken from so many, resulting in our mentally and financially poor society.

It is when we give in to society's demands that the demand for our individual self is weakened. Rather than trying our own route in life, we give up our freedom and identity to the highest bidder.

In life, as it may start at home or in school, it all leads to the same destination. Our own rules and lives get replaced with waiting for someone to give us a new task or a new route. College students hear repeatedly from the professor that their paper is due in a week, on top of the many others due as well. Before many of us know, it is time to drop all of our freedom and happiness.

The infamous question arises, "What do you want to do with your life." For many young kids, it is brushed off. The idea of college life is all that can be thought about. Those new friends that you are not forced to sit with like in high school. The future cannot be seen past what party is coming up.

It is a new carefree feeling that one can experience. As graduation nears, it is right back to thinking about your career. We begin to settle down and accept that it is time to focus on your "job", instead of yourself. This idea is always kept in the back of the head. It eats away until a job is chosen that is secure and can hopefully afford a new place in the nice side of town.

"Now entering the norm" becomes the only path we will know, and some have never even seen another path. Bills pile up, money is short, and every four years you are hoping a new president will fix it.

Life becomes nothing but wishing for the next thing. Little actually changes, except for the new problems we develop. Before you know it, your life has passed you by.

It is this eye opener that causes many to choose the entrepreneurial route. The 9-5 life is not sought after. If one really searches, you can find that this is just the preparation that modern day schools have taught.

From a young age, the training begins for the "norm". Regardless of who is to blame, school has become a restless time of clock staring and daydreaming. Rules became meaningless, unless we created them.

Vision how life was when we were all younger. When school ended, our day began. This freedom stuck by, and the need for more never left. The path we are on at a young age should guide us to our future. Instead, we become less like ourselves and more like the norm.

"For me personally, this training never got through to me. I did what I had to please everyone, only after we made the most of it."

College is much of the same without the long class days and stricter rules. The freedom is there, but the time is limited. Time will never be enough for our desires and goals. This idea is put in us early on. Playing it safe appeals to many as deep fears about failure pour in. For many, the risk is never as appealing as the reward.

This slight realization offers hope to our broken self and ultimately, broken world. The timeless saying that we are the change we want to see, has never had more of a powerful meaning. The world spins in a way that we are not pleased with because we walk down the opposite way.

The power to provide change comes with the change we make in ourselves. We can ask what went wrong with the world as soon as we find out what went wrong with ourselves. We are all equally responsible for the mistakes that occur every day. The very first question anyone should ask themselves is whether they like the person they are.

It is a life changing moment that so many refuse to address as they know the answer will hurt them. This ignorance only leads to anger boiling into hate. The hate comes from the self, but is directed at others.

The problem is planted by us. The only solution lies in addressing the mistakes that we made. Some questions are hardly found within oneself. "Why is this anger and hate present after doing everything that the norm has asked of?" is an example.

The self and the country experience major and difficult problems. Meanwhile, each has had an opportunity for a better outcome this whole time.

We are staring it in the eyes like fighters at a weigh-in. It is right in front of our face, but we either cannot see it or refuse to. The opportunity to better life ahead and create positive change comes from analyzing who we are. No matter how wrong or unfair the situation is, it is only up to us to find a way out. At this point, we must admit that.

This realization has already impacted so many. Every new entrepreneur the world produces met this truth in their journey and it's hard to turn back.

It lies within every success story that you will ever read. When you finally discover that you are your own provider of dreams coming true, the world is yours.

CHAPTER 9

GOOD FOR BUSINESS

"I'm not a businessman, I'm a business, man.

- Jay-Z

The method in which you choose to educate
yourself and find who you are at your current state will
be your greatest investment. It is also the most time
consuming. The idea to have self-love and look at life as
the most precious thing we have is the sole dream of
every member of the human race.

You will only be taught that by the person who
truly wants it, yourself. The prominent Jay-Z quote
scribed previously in the chapter accurately describes
every entrepreneur that has met great mental and
financial success.

Viewing yourself as its own business drowns out anything that holds you back. Drama, negativity, failure, or anything else that holds you back will cease to exist. Perhaps this makes the idea of self-education clearer. Self-education relates to whatever helps you grow, and you as a business.

"Without any idea as to who I was or what I should do with my life, I did know one thing. I wanted to live by my own lifestyle. I did not see why a person could not be happy, but also rich. So many in our world today are either mentally rich and financially poor, or financially rich but lack mental richness as well."

In a very watered down way, this is what has contributed to our broken society, country and world. Perhaps, in some innocent way that lies deep within ourselves, is the reason for the broken world. Perhaps, if more were mentally AND financially rich, we could end income inequality, poverty, and violence while living the wonderful life that we dreamt of.

The basis for our research stemmed from these ideas. What happened? Why is everyone so divided? Why are we struggling so hard to be a functioning society? How is the rich getting richer, while the poverty rate goes up?

While growing up, many do not live by "normal" circumstances. Instead, much of our creativity and freedom is already being manufactured for us. The hardest thing we search for in this life is what we will actually do with that life. Instead of searching for what will help us grow, others are redirecting us elsewhere.

It is seen in kids being told to go to school, to get a job that is safe and secure. Put most of your money in a 401k. Now, as many grow older, they start setting aside passions, dreams, and goals to focus on what society wants. The majority are not happy with the 9-5 route. With more of those jobs are not seeing growth in income, or AI replacing them altogether, it does not appear to be the safe route anymore.

Allowing others to direct our route will always be bad for business. This is where many choose to compromise.

"It was when I reached this perspective that I realized no one was learning real success. Many people were walking around mentally and financially poor searching for better answers in all the wrong places. It was then that I knew I was part of them as well. I had realized that I was part of my own problems. It was then, that I had to reroute and discover me."

Deep down inside of our minds we know the real solution is us. Each and every one of us can contribute to the solution, every single day. This also implies that deep down many see how we have been compromising our freedom to please others.

It can be seen, again, from an early age. This discourse causes many to become full of hate and anger. Whether it is directed at themselves or others can still have a harmful effect. There is rarely an occurrence of a mentally and financially rich individual that is full of hate or anger. Otherwise, their money means nothing. A poor mental state only weakens themselves and the innocent.

There is a surplus of people that maintain a good heart and still struggle in life. It is not because of laziness, or that they are empty-headed. We all know someone like this, and the truth is, many who struggle with great failures or difficulties are often the ones with the most potential.

"I began to question why such innocent and good-hearted people never got a break. It made me question how we got to a point where we have people living in poverty, while others are joining the new rich."

People are still not reaching their full potential, and we must bring it out of others. While it may not work to just share our wealth, we can share our knowledge.

"A big problem that I faced was finding the right tools to succeed in my life, in my way. My love for reading lead to my personal growth. It was especially growing with just the slightest gain in financial literacy."

"I started to see that school was never going to give me the tools to get out of poverty. I succeeded in school, but the biggest struggle was always a need to learn something more than what it ever taught us."

"I realized that if school was not going to teach me what I needed, then I would do it myself. This personal growth education taught me how to use my freedom, happiness and passion to obtain a rich life."

"I was discouraged about school and even many jobs that I had. I was not satisfied at the fact that I was there constantly, forced to prepare myself to perform the day to day tasks of a future job. The role of HR did not interest me as much as how to defeat poverty and mental health illnesses."

You're looking at where it all started. We have to change the world, but how? Before we ever asked others, we looked within. Somewhere deep down, we discovered that the only way to change the world for the better was to first change ourselves. One day, we looked in the mirror and asked ourselves a question. Would we like us through someone else's eyes? The number of revelations that came about multiplied.

"When I left the house, I instantly become the boss of my own life. I wanted people to see me as the change that people wanted. Performing this action is not as easy as many may think. This is especially true for people who have severe anxiety or self-doubt.

The reason we wrote this book is because we could not come to this free, happy, and rich life until we were officially shattered. We found ourselves over a very long time. Through the many failed attempts in life, we had finally succeeded. Looking back, it was the easiest solution to all of our problems.

We eventually found our path, after we finally realized that we were on someone else's path. We never chose to be going in the wrong direction, but somehow it happened. Once we started navigating our own path, we came to the conclusion that we had to spread this realization to others. We had bettered our lives and were ready to make a living off of it. We knew once we did, we could change other people in life. We had to start small. Changing the world does not happen overnight. It takes a lifetime. Accept that reality, and you can relax and start small.

Take the pressure off by realizing that you have time to progress. Understand that it will not be an overnight success. Until that jump comes, invest in yourself so you can be fully aware of your calling. Every day must be a new chance to learn.

You must constantly analyze the world and comprehend why things happen the way that they do. Inside every problem lies a solution. No problem has ever been too great to handle. This frequently starts with one person simply possessing an idea. From there, they develop, and so does the idea. Eventually, you are changing the world for the better. Analyzing is an imperative component to free yourself.

CHAPTER 10

THE ILLUSION OF TIME AND OUR CONTROL

"The past has no power over the present moment."

— Eckhart Tolle

For true success in life, as said before, mental-richness is required along with financially proficiency. Chasing money is a never ending cycle of insanity. You can never reach a limit, and it only causes one to lose what is important. Money has no value without knowledge. There will always be an endless supply of materials to purchase.

While money is endless, so is knowledge and personal growth. Obtaining knowledge should be the only growth that you need. With the right guidance and mindset, the money will follow close behind.

If one would chase knowledge instead of just possession, a healthier mental state can create a foundation for the financial state. Knowledge is not material. It is only space. It is space that betters you and others around you.

Self-growth creates the ethical leadership that many in the old rich do not maintain. Once you know who you are in your current state, you can observe others and what makes them who they are. In a way, everything we do involves another human. It is what prevents someone from being "self-made".

Familiarize yourself with the actions and words of others. Care for others' lives in the way you would care for yourself. Someone somewhere has knowledge that you do not have. Someone out there could also benefit from that knowledge. Small behaviors such as this can better a friend, family member, or the human race.

Let's boil down the single biggest issue this country faces that divides individuals in their own community. This issue breaks the heart and soul of this nation, not to mention that it is being disguised in politics.

We are left with the single idea that we have spent the last three years researching: Why are the rich getting richer and the poor getting poorer?

There will be a time and a place to dissect this 40 year-old issue, but let's begin by purely solving it. Let's first accept that we have the solutions. Politicians must do their job, but ultimately, we need to be the provider of the answer.

The puzzling question of why society is not getting any better has been misconstrued by our educators and elites.

We cannot take the academic or political side for the solution. We must take the business side. The issue of why the rich are getting richer and the poor are getting poorer is about money. The solution must also be money. It is the understanding of money and how the art of money has affected this whole problem. The simple understanding of money and the power of it can transform anyone's financial situation.

Owning the power that money gives the individual is infinite. This is not meant to be taken in a negative or corrupt way. We do not incorporate greed as well, which is a massive topic for discussion these days.

Individuals should know the power of being a self-employed person. We do not need more business majors, or even more college students at all. People are passionate and filled with positive energy. Many want a successful life that they are able to control.

We are as capable of creating our own life as any politician that we vote for. A lack of education in business and money holds many behind after they understand themselves.

It has caused generations to grow up unsuccessful and blame their failures on older generations. This cycle has been going on for quite some time and has not disappeared anywhere.

The issue comes down to what the rich understand that the poor do not. This issue becomes where to locate that information? Older generations may recommend college and a safe and secure job.

For the ones that do not take the entrepreneurial route, they are faced with tens of thousands of dollars in debt, with little hope of it disappearing. The whole route is losing its importance. Without financial education, ones debt will only increase.

Let us be the first to say that teachers, professors and politics are important fields to be involved in. We must not diminish their role in society. Education reform is essential, at whatever costs for the betterment of society. The ideas and knowledge that we learn defines how our future will transpire.

CHAPTER 11

MISGUIDED, NOT LOST

The act of being guided by another person other than yourself is poor for your business. Do not let anyone control your mental or financial state. Do not let life and those in it push you around. Too many have become dependent on others for their success. This is mostly seen in our need for college and policies. Demanding more from others instead of demanding more from yourself has become quite the norm.

This was never in the plan for our individual lives, yet here we are. Many who take their own path typically choose the entrepreneurial route for this reason. Working for others can make a person, such as an entrepreneur, question who they are and what worth their career has. Keeping this issue locked up inside leads to the weakening of the mind and no longer seeing the point of life.

Passions cannot be pushed aside for anything or anyone. As we age and compromise, the self suffers. How does one explain the anger that so many feel? It results from years of being led down a road not made for them, passions becoming the past, and the self getting more and more lost. The financial crisis that we face falls solely on us to fix. Many have not fixed their minds, and therefore, cannot fix their income.

Unfortunately, this is becoming who we are. It is seen every day. Anger, hate, and unhappiness. It stems from our path being left behind for the mistaken one. We are never lost, only misguided. The political divide that is too present has started from a lack of identity in individuals. The path has led us down one with no identity, resulting in hate, frustration, and division.

Individuality is shrinking due to ongoing social norms that take you off of your path. Being misguided for so long is causing many to feel as if they are lost with no chance of ever getting better. Society as a whole has been transformed by this type of thought process.

Discovering who is responsible and ready to take the blame for this phenomena is not important. Meanwhile, a way out is indeed possible. It is not fair to our world, or ourselves, to give up hope.

A hopeless, misguided soul is one that will never achieve a happy life, and achieve a wealthy status.

The first step in becoming a successful entrepreneur comes from their sense of self-love and self-respect. One is never truly free until the love and respect is there.

Self-love and freedom makes a person who they are. Without this, one is no longer a whole, but rather a part of a group that adds to the divide. They are warped to believe whatever the norm is before the self ever sees it through.

The self gets ignored and the reaction is filled with hate and anger. These two feelings originate in how we view ourselves. It is not the feeling of dislike in another person, but rather an instantaneous dislike in the self that had a purpose.

An additional crucial step of a successful entrepreneur is acquiring knowledge from jobs that you once had.

Even if you hate the job you have, always remember to keep striving for your dream career. Every job that you have has a take away that needs to be searched for. Until that day happens, prepare for the happiness with today's imperfect days.

Consistently criticizing the current chapter of your life will ultimately lead you to want the next thing. Periods of analyzing are needed to understand what can be altered in a positive way. You will forget to live until you finally realize that it is too late.

In reality it is never too late. It is why entrepreneurs are developed from all age groups. When someone is pursuing their goals, their "grind" means more than a number defining their age.

Once you finally make your jump, talk about it and be proud of it. This how you know you are finally on your own "grind."

Being on a grind is claimed by so many and easily misconstrued. The inner secrets of the grind are often never discovered, or found out in an unfavorable approach.

The negativity that people release when they hear the term "grind" may originate from all of their failure stories. Many of us prefer listening to failed stories rather than success because it is more appealing.

This is not to put anyone down. It is almost natural behavior. Once on the grind pursuing entrepreneurial goals, the failure stories will be thrown around a lot. While many throw them your way, accept this secret of the grind.

Taking every little thing too personally will only hurt yourself. It will hurt your grind and your sense of purpose can be distorted. Stick to your grind and remember to never take things too serious. You are approaching the later stages of your journey by completing these actions.

Also, remember to have fun with it. Talk about the grind. Be honest with yourself and others. You are on your new journey. Everyone can know without any pressure if you accept the natural order of things. It is one small step that leads to another. No matter how long it may take, our final destination is there.

Every day of your life should consist of finding time for your grind. When the day is over and you have put your head on the pillow, ask yourself whether you were satisfied with your day and maintaining your grind. If not, do better tomorrow. Ultimately, we should never become satisfied until success has been reached. This is how to stay hungry, and have fun with it, at the same time.

As many entrepreneurs will tell you, one will never learn this in traditional schooling. The education you pursue will be your way to a higher financial state.

Once richness is added into our mental state, we take action on the financial state as well. This is all that one needs to know to succeed in this ever changing world.

It is uncomplicated to see how we only need our education and ourselves to succeed. The liability after high school education is becoming more recognizable and seen by an increased number of people.

Our education system is currently taking us in the completely wrong direction. It is a sad and scary time when this can be said, but it is still sadly true. This is the realization that the new rich sees. A college education is no longer the same value as it once was because of the amount of new rich entrepreneurs that did not need one.

This can explain why so many schools are losing funds and student debt is increasing at an alarming rate. Income inequality will only become worse as the years go on. Our only hope lies in a secondary degree and the politicians that we vote for, but does it really need to be that way? How are we producing more millionaires than ever before while income equality hurts so many? The answer lies in the "Demand" for change.

"The Demand for Change" will only be met when we search for the truth, no matter how hard the truth is on us. We are in demand for better education, better and more ethical business, and more money in the pockets of every individual. We are in a demand for a better life that is created by nobody but ourselves.

There is also a demand to be better. The first step in acquiring a better education is learning from the accurate people. We always look for the best of things: the best situation, the best person, and the best life for one another. Perhaps, this is where we are directed by society and their norms rather than being guided by our own path.

What will work for one will not work for another. We need less of what is "best", and more of what is right. We must provide and maintain the right tools to succeed in the future. It needs to be precise for where we are headed in order to produce more self-sufficient entrepreneurs. This means that there is a hard truth we are missing. There are too many of us that are not taking our own path or living our own lives that we are blessed to have.

There is one demand for the individual self, the demand for their own lifestyle. It is never going to be about the money anymore. Corruption and greed can be phased out. We can focus on what keeps us happy rather than letting our ego verbalize for us.

Discovering the importance of leaving the norm may pose as a challenge for some. It certainly was for us.

The norm must be abandoned to make room for your own path. A rich and fulfilling life is awarded to anyone (from any background) that is willing to complete the process and take the steps. Money and happiness does not discriminate. In fact, it sees passion, values, hard work, and the will to learn in a person.

Overcome the hurdle and figure out that we control our own path. Any mistakes we experience are caused by us. However, we are also the solution.

It is often heard from everyday people that who you are or where you come automatically puts you at a disadvantage. We know that the world is not, and never was, perfect.

Repeatedly viewing your "failures" as a lesson for growth puts one at an advantage. The only "advantage" one speaks of is a simple rerouting of the mindset. It is why so many with a harder upbringing lead very rich and successful lives as entrepreneurs. What they saw as their "advantage", you must see as yours as well.

Your struggles must be looked at as an advantage that others do not have. People with the hardest lives and obstacles have gone on to achieve great things.

These success stories are heard of in famous athletes, entertainers, and successful business people.

At this point, acknowledge your struggle and past and use this as a motivator. Your story can be used as a way to motivate others. The more you succeed, the more of a following you will pick up. Your life is essentially a book that others will read about one day. Your first priority needs to be how to let go of the past and move forward.

Imagine a simple task such as walking. You are moving constantly and do not look back. Life is a series of metaphors. When simple features are applied to your life path, there is nothing that can stop you.

This is not to change you or open up some new ideas to you. There is no selling or ideology in this. You are simply awakening your inner-self and conquering your own world.

In every issue we face, the anger and hate that is buried deep down can be replaced. We hold the key to our future and lives. While we unconsciously seek others for the key, our present-self is just waiting to come out and succeed.

Allow for your true identity to awaken. You have a passion and a purpose, and with that, you can conquer the world. Our failure originates from the fact that we have not conquered our own world and are living in someone else's.

You are being lead down the wrong path. Accept that you are lost, broken, and poor. The other path is the one you should be enjoying. This path is the one where you control your freedom, happiness, and riches.

CHAPTER 12

MIRROR

How can we believe in the world when we cannot even believe in ourselves? Instead of waiting and hoping for someone to come along and save us, let's just make the assumption that we are going to be the one to do it. Therefore, we have no other option.

It is once an entrepreneur accepts that there is no other option, that they can begin their journey. A major step in making your jump is accepting this reality.

This all circles back to seeking a happy, free, and rich life. Now that you can accept that those three things are only obtained by you, make the change.

There are good and bad events in the world. Everyone has their struggles, that is always a given. The ideas that we control how we perceive life gives hope to it.

Take for example how a negative situation carries energy through different people. The negativity that has caused our society to become divided and poor must have an end or a solution. It is the darkest of times that presents the most opportunity.

If one were to view every great event that has taken place throughout the world, dark and bitter times are stored deep down included in that success story.

It is truly amazing what one individual can accomplish through a richer mindset. Whether you are experiencing your darkest days or still feel the effects of those times, take action in changing the energy.

Put yourself in these shoes. You are facing the most feared and dark time of your life. What on Earth should you do? Look for the smallest things to change your mood. No one ever just wakes up one day with a body full of hope. Pinpoint those minor, sometimes forgotten about, times of the day that you enjoy and feel your passion most present.

Negativity and positivity are complete opposites. It is a fact that there must be another side to the current negative feelings and energy. When you take small steps to replace the current negativity, eventually the weight of the scale in your mind will shift.

Eluding the feeling of sadness or pain is tough, but it does not have to consume us. When we view our life as a whole, it is easy to view all the things that we do not have, or cannot even reach. This has consumed so many to collectively create a poor minded and financially poor society.

It is how and why we must create a new generation of entrepreneurs. It is a must to start small, and start now. No one can fix everything overnight, but that does not mean we shouldn't try.

One must be able to view the negativity and analyze it. Never accept it. Search for an opportunity to make positive light out of any situation you face, no matter how small. In fact, it is even better if we only make small progress in our lives.

The opportunities that lie for a rich life should amaze us. The amount of negative energy that surrounds us has gotten so powerful. It has caused the massive divide we see.

The political divide has only originated from the divide between the rich and the poor. The income gap has caused people on the same side, in the same position, to fight each other.

An idea that stays true in our current lives is that the rich continue to get richer while the poor stay poor.

People fail to see that this is the root of every major issue today. One simple issue (a lack of mental and financial education) has led to the massive divide that we see. A poor mental and financial state leads to violence, and there seems to be way too much of that. We are aware of how bad things have gotten without going into every event.

It is time to get back to the root of the problem. People have become more mentally and financially poor over the years. It is now time to stop the blame on others and solve it ourselves.

True success corresponds with how emotionally intelligent one is. Mental richness is only step one.

The second step uses the gift of mental strength to become financially rich. "It is in my opinion that a person possessing strong mental health can achieve any and all things that they want."

We can all do well and contribute to the success and richness of the world, but first we have to do that for ourselves. We all know how a better mental health initiative will fix one problem. Now, let's figure out how and why a rich financial state is the second step to the better life we desire.

CHAPTER 13

REASON FOR INCOME INEQUALITY

Often, some of the most educated students have very little financially literacy. They are educated, but in the wrong ways. It has misguided so many. It might be non-traditional, but the only true intelligence one should obtain is a healthy emotional and financial education.

We are all different in major ways. We are different in the way we were brought up, and also how "smart" we are told we are. However, there are a few aspects in which we are all connected by: our passions and our freedom.

When it comes down to the simplest of terms, turning our passion into great riches is the ultimate goal. Achieving freedom involves living a life based on your own terms and finding peace in whatever it is that you do each day.

The traits of happy, free, and rich are the most desired traits that we seek. Take a glance at your own life. Ask yourself a simple question. "Why aren't I satisfied with this life?"

We could essentially solve every major world problem if we just focused on becoming mentally and financially rich. A new, rich generation of entrepreneurs is society's life-saver. The solution lies in each and every one of our hands. We are all in demand. We are in demand to become the next rich entrepreneur.

It is simple, and the answer is the demand for more entrepreneurs. There is a demand for a new way of life and how we live that life.

The ideas and topics that our energy is put into greatly matters. It is apparent in our media outlets and perceptions of the current state of the world that we are craving negative energy. This forms from allowing emotions, specifically negative emotions, to define who we are.

Energy in the wrong emotions leads to a false identity. As we lose hope in ourselves and the world around us, we allow our negative vibes to take over. This is where much of our low self-esteem and insecurity originates. Instead of absorbing positive vibes and letting them push us to meet our true identity, we have now become the negative energy that we release.

It is hard to imagine that all of the country's problems could be solved so effortlessly, but take a few things into consideration. Allow for the mind to open up and enable a new idea with a positive vibe to flow through it. You may find that you have never been truly successful because you have never believed that you could through positive vibes.

The energy that you carried never allowed for a chance of success. That positive energy could have allowed you to think positively and make it out of any barrier you have ever faced.

MONEY IS DEAD

Money is dead. Sure, this headline might already seem to have zero chance of ending well. It's not as bad as it sounds. As the rich get richer and the poor get poorer, people continue to lose hope. It has gotten so bad that we have searched long and hard for answers in the wrong places.

Although the idea of money dying sounds depressing, this is more of an informative message as to why these things occur. Before we can ever understand why the gap between rich and poor expands, we must first look at how we got here.

Money is not what it once was. In fact, it had become completely worthless. When money changed, people and education did not. The result has been an ongoing depression that seems to be getting worse as we lose hope and search for answers that many do not even have.

"We can prosper once again, I believe that. We know we must be the change to a better life. The hard part is knowing where to start."

"I first discovered this truth when searching for an answer as to why and how the rich got richer and so many people I know got poorer as the years went by. What I was missing this whole time was the main topic of discussion: money. I realized that I did not know how money worked. The schools I attended were not giving answers and I knew I must find it myself on my own power."

How we got to this point in America is not as complicated as it sounds and the fix is even easier. Let's first understand that money has no value. It sounds crazy to some, but ask the rich how it appears and they may agree.

"I am far from saying we all just need to be grossly rich and full of greed. However, I am saying that we must search for the truth where it lies. A lot of events happened to get us to this point. Money lost its worth and has resulted in a dysfunctional society that sees very little hope."

Our intentions are to guide us back on the right path, one that searches for solutions rather than the next fight. We must start somewhere. We are in a prosperous land full of opportunity. Before we can better the country, let's understand how and why we have gotten to this crazy time that we live in.

CHAPTER 14

HOW BAD IS IT?

The definition of an economic derivative can be misinterpreted. A derivative is a value that is reliant upon the assets that one owns to make them money.

Let's keep this very short and simple. There are over $1 quadrillion in derivatives floating out there. In 2007, when the economy crashed and the United States suffered a recession, there were roughly $700 trillion in derivatives. When these types of derivatives (sometimes referred to as "bubbles") pop, they crash the economy. The poor and middle class suffer, and many times the rich get richer.

While this all sounds terribly unfair, it is actually very straightforward to see how the rich get richer and the poor get poorer. More importantly, the reason comes down to who understands money and how it works.

In this chapter, you will fully understand how the rich have been getting richer and how you can become part of a new rich.

There has been an incredible amount of confusion on what happened to America. What truly happened to America and why does the fighting and division make zero sense?

The answer lies in you and where you get your information.

"I had decided to participate in crafting this book to provide a warning. The current bubble has over a quadrillion dollars floating around. To put this in perspective (other than the fact that you may never have heard of the word quadrillion), this amount is over 20 times the entire world's gross domestic product (GDP)."

If (let's hope we are not predicting the future here) this happens, it would cause a collapse that would make the Great Depression seem like nothing.

The reason cannot be found in our politicians or our schools. Experts of entrepreneurship have spoken the same words. These are the people living a happy, free, and rich life.

When we wipe out all of the distractions and dividers, we are left with a very financially illiterate group of people. While this is not a specific person's fault, other than the very people who taught us the wrong things for so long, we must accept that we have always been in control as to who is in charge. It lies within us as individuals.

To understand and grasp the point, we will start in the years of 1933 and 1971. These two pivotal years and their relationship with gold is all we ever need to know about why the rich get richer and the poor get poorer.

We will address the series of events that led to America's current status. We do not place any blame or take a stance to support a side. We are simply here to provide the truth. The quotes around some of the headlines is to show that it is history, nothing can be done, and we must only let go of the past and look ahead. Allow yourself to learn and understand new education about money, based on historical events. Money is very independent. It does not go where you go. Instead, we must be the ones to chase money and learn its ways.

At the conclusion of this book, after what you have heard and can confirm, is there a need to change? Is there a need for a better world before it is too late? With that, the answer is up to you.

"FDR AND THE GOLD STANDARD"

On June 5, 1933, President Franklin Delano Roosevelt (FDR) took the United States off of the gold standard. Gold was the system in which we determined the value of our money.

The United States had been on the gold standard since 1879. After June 5, 1933, creditors no longer were taking gold as a form of payment.

The Great Depression was one of the darkest times in the country, and even the world. Many lived in poverty and just as many were plainly broken. World leaders capitalized on the fears, and soon citizens feared of fascists and socialists taking over the world. When the big banks were failing, many people started collecting gold.

This gave meaning to money. It allowed the United States to live within their means. It also meant that the government could not just print money whenever they pleased, like they do today.

Within FDR's "First Hundred Days", he declared a nationwide ban to halt the chaos and fear of the citizens that the banks were failing.

The president also banned the banks from paying out gold to anyone. This was all done with the intention to inflate the money supply, with the intent of preventing a massive economic downturn. Other countries had gone and done the same thing, since the Great Depression hurt the global economy as well.

It was in April 1933, one month after announcing the ban, that the president instructed all gold coins and certificates to be turned over in exchange for other money.

Gold has been existent longer than humans have been on Earth. As humans created societies in which transactions need to be made, gold was always the choice for their currency. While it is almost impossible to determine when humans first found gold, some of the earliest traces come from around 40,000 BC.

Many were attracted to gold for its metal coloring and the natural feel of it. Thousands of years after existing, gold was morphed into a solid form rather than the soft form it once was.

It was not until the ancient Egyptians created this solid matter that humans used gold as a symbol of great wealth.

As gold was passed down through the years of different civilizations, it remained a universal language for wealth and as a form of currency.

It was then that Great Britain created the "Gold Standard". The British were the first set this standard and the United States were not too far behind. The U.S. followed Britain's steps again during the Great Depression when they dropped the gold standard.

The Mint and Coinage Act of 1792 was passed in the United States to establish a mint and regulated the coins of the country.

Most Americans are familiar with the gold rush in the 1800s. There is even a football team named after the prospectors who traveled to mine gold. Gold has always been a symbol of wealth and it gave value to the U.S. dollar. It was about a decade after gold was found in California that Treasury Secretary Salmon Chase printed the very first United States paper currency.

Following these monumental acts, in 1900 President William McKinley signed the Gold Standard Act. This act also allowed for silver to count as a form of monetary standard. This lead to the creation of the Federal Reserve in 1913. Their job at the Federal Reserve System was to stabilize gold and currency values.

While this was a huge change in the way money was given its value, it was still on a gold standard. Gold was still on the Federal Reserve balance sheets. During the Depression, the Feds had a massive increase of assets of gold, allowing them to inflate the money supply. It was also during this time that the government put the price of gold at $35 an ounce. Things had really changed and led to the confusion we live in today. In August of 1971, President Richard Nixon officially took the United States off of the gold standard. This then led to what is called Fiat Money, or "fake money."

As the government just prints money at the rate that they do, how could money hold any value? Money is nothing anymore and the rich have discovered this. It is why they keep getting richer while the ones who fail to see this continue to fall into poverty. Money is only used for building assets, not saving.

This is exactly how the new rich have been created, even though more and more are falling into poverty.

CHAPTER 15

THE TIME IS NOW

"Experience tells you what to do; confidence allows you to do it."

-Stan Smith

Before you can ever achieve your goals and achieve the ultimate freedom, you must become the CEO of your life. Business is a part of our everyday lives. Essentially, we are running a business within ourselves.

Here is another question for you to ponder about. How can you advance your personal growth, build a business, remain ethical, and achieve great wealth? We will tell you how.

Life is a series of lessons to become the best version of yourself that there is. We are not growing like we should be. It might be the result of being misguided and leaving behind the self-confidence to get to the top. It also means that, as a society, we cannot progress.

This has resulted in the economic and political turmoil we are far too familiar with. Before those problems can be solved, we must use the craft of starting a business for crafting our minds.

Deciphering your life and understanding who you are always comes first. Remember: there is one person in charge of your life. While it is true, we will need others to succeed. They are as crucial to your success as you are, but in the end, you are making decisions for yourself.

Look for others who are trying to grow and or need to grow at a faster rate. Look at those around you as a way to learn and grow your "business". Use what you have learned to advance yourself.

What is "selfish" to one mindset, is actually a mindset for growth and success. This takes many off of the track that society has put them on.

Your life is very similar to a business, as there are millions and millions of employees, but only one CEO. The executive decision maker takes into account other's thoughts and analysis, but chooses what they believe to be the best for the business.

Achieving this only occurs by looking at every member of society as a part of your business. Just as you are a part of theirs, in the end, they make the final choice in their life. The same goes for you. A person who is typically distraught or always angry is just on a different side of the same coin. Their strong emotions that have been lashed out at the world are outcomes from their lack of freedom and happiness.

The people mentioned above are not the CEO of their life, but rather the custodian. Custodians are crucial to our daily business, as is every profession, but you never want to be the custodian of your own life. Take the time to acknowledge that you are a background character in someone else's life.

No matter what happens, the story is about them. Rarely, actions are done as a personal attack on someone else. Rather, the person has decided to make a decision that betters them and their own life.

We all do this in our everyday lives, but when it happens to us, our ego steps in. You cannot be the CEO of someone else's life, just as you cannot be the custodian of your own.

The decisions you make are coming from a selfish desire to succeed and be happy.

Your decision to be happy will not always please others. Once they see this and can move past it, they will now be able to do it for themselves.

Nothing should be taken personally. Nobody should have the power to make your decisions. In the long-run, we control our feelings, and thus, control our attitude towards the situation.

Be certain to stay present throughout your process. Remember to come back to your surroundings and always keep your loved ones close. At the conclusion, there are more lives depending on your success than just your own. Your role is to better yourself, along with everyone else as well. We have the power to make a colossal impact on those we care most about.

Keep in mind that you are not working up a chain to become CEO. You are creating your own path to your own business.

Ultimately, this should lead to a life where you create your own business to govern. This business is lead from your passion and maintained through your morals and ethics.

Recall that it is not all about us and our desires. Considering we are all sharing the same planet, we must work together. Without unity, one's personal wealth means very little.

Frequently, we observe people going broke while trying to look rich. Many think rich and have rich creativity, but few are willing to take the correct actions to become rich.

If you are creating more liabilities than you can pay for, forget about ever becoming rich. Possessing one source of income that is only earned from multiple liabilities will hold you down more than any other barrier in life.

It is very easy to see how poverty has not been fading away for many. The fact that we talk about the importance of education, but somehow forget financial education in a capitalist country, is baffling. In order to stop ourselves from pointing fingers, let's stick to the facts.

Money, at a young age, should be coming out of your wallet as an investment towards your future. This includes education that comes from outside of a classroom.

"I have always felt puzzled when I notice people complaining about spending $30 on a book, but will spend over $400 that they do not have for a material possession."

Rather than mimic those with riches, work like them. It is the visibility to see that anyone can achieve riches that is the real reason for being rich. In the end, it will not matter who you are, where you come from, or what you look like. Think of the successful people that come to mind at this moment. All that matters is that you live with a rich attitude.

Perhaps, we need to embrace one another and all of the different and beautiful cultures that exist. Perhaps, we need to finally be true to our values and look past what is on the surface. We should all be judged for our ethics, how rich we think, and the work ethic to achieve freedom, happiness, and riches.

CHAPTER 16

SIMPLER TIMES AWAIT

"In a time of destruction, create something."

- Maxine Hong Kingston

Whether it is income inequality or the student debt crisis, the way in which we talk about and handle such discussions has led to the political divide that is evident in today's news.

What we think divides us (which is our political opinions) is actually a cover up for the larger issue of the divide between the rich and poor.

If we can accept the fact that we must reform the way we perceive things, we can make the poor richer. Student debt is a crisis, but a better long term solution is not to minimize it, but to ignore bad debt.

We should have an expectation of noticing more entrepreneurs and people who experience the rags to riches story. The ones who have succeeded in business and making money, all in an ethical way, need to be those that we learn from.

Taking advice from something or somebody experiencing the same misfortunes as you only causes more problems. This has been what we have seen in the classrooms and politics for years. Again, we can either place blame or let go of that past. Letting go will only benefit our chances of success.

The major issue that we face is the way in which one looks at an undesirable situation. They let that negativity change their mindset for the worst.

It is also important to take into consideration the people who have the right mentors in their lives. At such an early age, we develop a basis of thinking and ideology based on the people around us. Some of us have the right people teaching us ethics and shaping our minds. This can breed the right person who exemplifies what morals should be.

As a society, we must not demean those that could not control who shaped their minds. We must embrace success and ethics, regardless of whether it was considered easier for them. Even if you were not born with the perfect role model by your side, you must find it.

"For me, I found it in books. It is up to you how you find this role model or inspiration to mold your mind. You must search the world until you find what makes you happy and successful."

"I believe, especially in my own personal life, that having a rough start and having all the odds stacked against you gives you more of a chance to succeed. I have always had to work a little harder than others. The more times that I failed in life, the more successful I was inevitably becoming. The barriers and struggles I have faced in my life has given me an advantage that many may not ever see."

Viewing struggles as a blessing is rare. Accepting that the odds are stacked against you can only lead to a poor life.

"Therefore, I have viewed my struggles as a blessing. It has made me realize that some see dust, others prefer to see diamonds."

It's all about how to turn that problem into a solution. This may be a skill that some are born with. For the rest of them, they must scratch tooth-and-nail to get to this point in their life. It shows how strong you are and blossoms a remarkable trait that only a select few have.

Many would agree that it takes time and effort to achieve the ethical behavior that is expected. Numerous children are taught to think through a tremendously narrow angle. This leads to a complete downfall later in their life.

This is a very conventional way of thinking that continues through high school and for many, even during their college years. We are ingrained at a young age that we live in a society that ultimately prevents the individual from reaching their full potential because they never grow themselves.

This leads to never truly understanding how to achieve success and being able to better determine what is right and wrong (or ethical and unethical).

Our first step to achieving success and remaining ethical is to solely focus on ourselves. There are too many horrible events that plague our world. People have been oppressed for too long.

So, it may sound selfish to focus on oneself as society has longed kept our true selves locked away.

"There is logic involved, and I always ask myself how I could ever have changed the world if I first did not change myself. This goes for every single human being, whether their past has been easy or difficult. The only way to envision how to solve the problem is to solve our own first, then share that knowledge.

This is a form of non-formal education that is not taught in your schools, yet some still carry it. We should never accept what we have in life. No matter how tough, recall others who may have had it worse and break away from the thought that it is too hard for you.

FEEL DIFFERENT AND EMBRACE THE JOURNEY

Feeling different often brings one down. Feeling different in more settings than feeling normal, can almost always destroy self-confidence.

This is freedom and passion that has not been seen in way too long. Now more than ever, we need that passion and persistence. No one else will help us. This is where we realize that the best way to beat the system is to be free. You are your own boss and that includes having the values and morals that come with the responsibility of being in charge. When every one of us has that rich mindset, not only are we successful, but so is everyone else around us.

The pioneers of American history were the bridge that connected a divided country. They were the perfect fit for both sides. They understood how to be free, happy, and live a rich life.

It is the attention and fame that, as humans, we desire. The ultimate goal in life is to be financially secure while being able to see past the money.

Every person you will come across in your life can be an instrumental part of the whole journey. Analyze others as you would yourself. You cannot find what separates you if you are only searching for the bridge that connects yourself with the other person.

Perceiving the values and ethics that others own attracts us to the person that shares a similar path as us. It is the basis for why successful people emphasize the need for a strong team. When analyzing others, there is no way to criticize or compete on a personal level with another person.

FINAL

FOLLOW THAT PASSION

The act of grinding and crafting your passion means to work nonstop. Work at anytime and anyplace to achieve the desired passion.

Humans are capable of so much more than their minds tell them. Businesses do not need to contain hundreds or thousands of dollars to launch. So much in our world has changed, yet the things we learn has not.

School has become a funnel that flows through the rat race. The 9-5 is being programmed into you until you forget what your passion is.

"I have a fondness for education. Attending college changed our lives. Education reform will single handedly solve 100% of our problems. The material that needs to be addressed in these institutions should be teaching ideas of our new and changed world."

A child that is only educated at school is not an educated child. It takes half of that formal education, and the other half comes from self-education.

Instead, we have seen years of full formal education and minimal self-education. Great leaders of our country understood this better than anyone.

"For too long, the individual self has been at war with what society expects of that self. I believe that all of the tensions, along with economic and environmental uncertainty, can be handled properly if we realize that we need more productivity, in ourselves and in business."

The only thing that connects every single person in the world, is that we all desire freedom, happiness, and a richer life.

The reason not everyone sees this is because we have been forced into groups that only separate us, rather than unite. Viewing life through those stages of happy free, and rich will result in letting go of reasons to hate or hurt.

The world is full of different people and groups that are all in search of these three principles. For so long, people have tried to unite us through the wrong methods. In many instances, they have done more harm than good.

Analyze every popular group in our world. The ideas for unity are there, but the approach is not quite effective.

Who is responsible for how far you make it in this world? The answer is you. You are the only person or thing that can stop you from succeeding.

You can't expect time to be on your side. Get on time's side. We are all the same in the aspect that we are given the same amount of time throughout our day.

What truly separates the rich from the poor is how they spend their time. This works for both the mentally poor and financially poor. The world essentially is the same to every one of us. The only thing that is different is how we perceive it. Thinking that you have all the answers is poor-minded. A truly educated person understands that they never need to be the smartest person in the room.

When this breaks down with being self-rich, you can utilize what makes you happy and free as a means to make money. Rather than seeing the world as getting poorer and scarier, view it as an opportunity to end it.

Just by focusing on your passion, dreams, and your grind, you can rise above the problem and be your own solution. We are given problems in life, but we must have the tools to fix it.

Live in the moment or the moment is gone. Waiting around for something to happen is going to consume your whole life. Knowing what you want to do and having the energy and desire to do it will leave two desirable outcomes to occur. You can either get to work or simply talk without any action.

There is an opportunity every single day for you to better yourself. The majority of us allow these opportunities to pass us and wait for the next opportunity to come around, whenever that will be.

It is a common habit for us humans to rely on others to do actions for us. We wait for a moment where others initiate the actions, then we follow. It is often felt as uncomfortable if you are the only person doing something.

Picture this: you are at a party and your favorite song comes on. You feel the urge to dance and just have fun, but everyone is standing around. We don't want to be the first ones to start dancing and have all eyes on us. We don't want to be the outcast of the party. Somebody has got to be the first one to start dancing. This person is going to remain calm and nonchalant because nobody else is dancing, although they would love to be.

We need to make the realization that it doesn't matter what others think. If you want to dance and that is your song, dance.

If you want to be happy, free, and rich but nobody else around you is making that change, what are you going to do? You will either live your life or live theirs. Those other people are going to be living the same life for many years to come. They have not come to the realization that their life is on the wrong path, but you have.

Los Angeles, London, Shanghai, Rome, and Sydney. Those are just some of the amazing places out there in this world that the majority of us cannot ever experience. Freedom restrictions and money issues ultimately affect your happiness.

"If we didn't make this jump and transition in thinking, I think that I would have been stuck in the same area that I've lived in my entire life. I would not get the chance to see any other cultures, landmarks, or history in this world that we live in. It is a shame, but some of us have such a restricted view on the Earth.

Now that you have become the CEO of your life, a leader to others, and no longer possess a "normal" mindset, you are training yourself to constantly stay on your path with a rich mind. This simple adjustment will allow all other perspectives to change in a more visible way. It is this confidence mixed with a richer perspective that allows you to see more opportunities during difficult times. It is this free feeling that makes having the weight of the world on your shoulders less stressful as you start walking down your path.

Your passion has always been in front of your face. You are free, you are happy, and now you can put that together and achieve great riches. Congratulations.

9 7 8 1 0 8 2 7 5 5 7 5 0